Hebai Marketing Research Institute

Nine Steps to Own the Job You Want

Nine Steps to Own the Job You Want

------First Disclosure of Traps Behind Recruitment

Author: **Hebai**
Friday, 16 August 2019

Recommended resources

----

https://amzn.to/2ZXoBIC
SAFEST Non Toxic Alphabet Puzzle Mat
Http://tomhua.com/cn/v/aff/aff.php?affid=17571
E-commerce treasure box
Http://wischina.cn/dvd/?affid=17571
World Internet Summit full video DVD
Http://wischina.cn/faba/lp2/?affid=17571
Send Bar Enterprise Edition
Http://www.ctrip.com/?AllianceID=1080785&sid=2061295&ouid=&app=0101F00
Ctrip

The cosmetics store sales speech (electronic version), which was first revealed, immediately improved the overall quality of store employees, and the sales of 500+ stores surged by more than 50%...
https://k.weidian.com/zVbKtM6A

Beauty salon front store backyard extension method collection (electronic version), so that the store no longer lacks customers, immediately upgrade store customers 50+ monthly
 https://k.weidian.com/bLbPpL4j

If you don't know this technology in the future, what I want to say is that your business will be very difficult. It can be said that this technology is the fastest money-making skill in the world. If you don't understand it, you can only blame God for unfairness every day. Why is the situation as I said? Click to get:
Https://share.lizhiweike.com/channel/522649?st=sharelink&inviter_id=66402134&share_platform=app

Chuanglan 253 Cloud Service
Http://cps.253.com/redirect/url?did=386&rid=0&jump=http://zz.253.com/site/register.html
Susie shop https://m.sudian178.com/#/weex/gift-list?investCode=266331545&isShare=1&from=singlemessage
PS Tutorial Super Compilation [1000 episodes of Champion]
https://study.163.com/course/introduction/1442008.htm?share=1&shareId=1397540243

AI Tutorial Super Compilation [500+ Champion Class]
(https://study.163.com/course/introduction/1003241018.htm?share=1&shareId=1397540243

AE Tutorial Super Compilation [400+ Champion Class]
(https://study.163.com/course/introduction/1005103011.htm?share=1&shareId=1397540243

With Jian Qi Xuecai
(https://study.163.com/course/introduction/1003418002.htm?share=1&shareId=1397540243

Easy to learn hand-drawn for the workplace plus points
(https://study.163.com/course/introduction/1003373019.htm?
share=1&shareId=1397540243

26 PPT practical classes thoroughly open the production
thinking
(https://study.163.com/course/introduction/1006225007.htm?
share=1&shareId=1397540243

Product Manager - Methodology + Actual Combat
(https://study.163.com/course/introduction/1003240007.htm?
share=1&shareId=1397540243

Soft Text Master - Marketing Copywriting Cheats
(https://study.163.com/course/introduction/1665014.htm?shar
e=1&shareId=1397540243

How does the income from wages go from 0 to 100,000 per
month
(https://study.163.com/course/introduction/1005577007.htm?
share=1&shareId=1397540243

Efficient learning: Cheats for double the value of the workplace
(https://study.163.com/course/introduction/1004627006.htm?
share=1&shareId=1397540243

How to effectively improve your workplace influence
(https://study.163.com/course/introduction/1005530009.htm?
share=1&shareId=1397540243

MBA management class entrance exam (logical series)
weakened strengthen

(https://m.ke.qq.com/course/434685?saleToken=1726006&sale
Link&from=h5link

[MBA PubMed English II (translation and writing)](https://m.ke.qq.com/course/432482?saleToken=1726007&saleLink&from=h5link)
(https://m.ke.qq.com/course/432482?saleToken=1726007&sale
Link&from=h5link

[2019 Institutional Public Basic Knowledge Innovation Course](https://m.ke.qq.com/course/433170?saleToken=1726008&saleLink&from=h5link)
(https://m.ke.qq.com/course/433170?saleToken=1726008&sale
Link&from=h5link

[188 sentences of universal travel](https://m.ke.qq.com/course/434061?saleToken=1726013&saleLink&from=h5link)
(https://m.ke.qq.com/course/434061?saleToken=1726013&sale
Link&from=h5link

["Standard Japanese 1" full course](https://m.ke.qq.com/course/402122?saleToken=1726016&saleLink&from=h5link)
(https://m.ke.qq.com/course/402122?saleToken=1726016&sale
Link&from=h5link

[Seoul Korean Extraordinary Series Elementary (TOPIK1~TOPIK2)](https://m.ke.qq.com/course/402349?saleToken=1726018&saleLink&from=h5link)
(https://m.ke.qq.com/course/402349?saleToken=1726018&sale
Link&from=h5link

[German original textbook "Begegnungen" famous teacher (A2)](https://m.ke.qq.com/course/413014?saleToken=1726023&saleLink&from=h5link)
(https://m.ke.qq.com/course/413014?saleToken=1726023&sale
Link&from=h5link

[AEIS/IELTS/TOEFL English exam preparation will be grammatical](https://m.ke.qq.com/course/421352?saleToken=1726026&saleLink&from=h5link)
(https://m.ke.qq.com/course/421352?saleToken=1726026&sale
Link&from=h5link

The National Second Construction Examination Management is
full of the 2004 issue

(https://m.ke.qq.com/course/433298?saleToken=1726030&sale
Link&from=h5link

Zero-based piano speed learning 10 songs for 100 minutes
(https://study.163.com/course/introduction/1006551009.htm?
share=1&shareId=1397540243

Zero-based yoga stretching, giving a fake neck
(https://study.163.com/course/introduction/1004850001.htm?
share=1&shareId=1397540243

7 minutes fat burning exercise - 28 days full version
(https://study.163.com/course/introduction/1005229016.htm?
share=1&shareId=1397540243

Freelance photographer
http://163.lu/QZ4G73

Real Estate Data Analyst
http://163.lu/xNYfY1

Machine Learning Engineer
http://163.lu/oqoGu0

New Media Video Director
http://163.lu/PfMMl4

table of Contents

It's a long way to find a job. How should I start?Where is the guiding light for famous enterprises?How to say goodbye to a boring resume filled with experience?How to avoid the result of no news from Haitou resume?How to prevent interviews with nothing to say but fear?Do you want to know where you lost the failed interview?Do you want to know about the recruitment process of the enterprise?Do you want to know all kinds of psychological logic of the interviewer?Do you want more job interviews?Do you want to hold on to your favorite Offer?If you do encounter these problems on your way to a job, and if you really read this beloved work, I am sure I can help you solve all the above problems.As a career coach with 10 years of experience in reading people and personally guiding 1000+ interns and new employees, I am committed to providing the most direct and effective help to new employees who are interested in entering the career. Whether it is personal career orientation, resume packaging, interview response skills, or promotion of career ability, you will gain a lot of reference methods by reading this book.This book is most suitable for readers: students who are used to taking the lead and preparing for the future.There is an urgent need to know the graduates who are looking for jobs.Those who are already in the workplace and wish to advance and are ready to change jobs.This book not only introduces you to specific theoretical knowledge of the workplace and effective job search methods, but also shows you a lot of specific recruitment, interview cases and fresh career stories, striving to make the originally boring job search trip interesting and vivid, so that you can observe the career path with ease and confidence, win opportunities for the future and realize your career dreams.Of course, you may have a little doubt-there are so many job-hunting books on the market at present. It seems that each book is called "treasure book" and "secret book". What are the advantages and characteristics of that book compared with other books?This book will not only talk about how to do a resume, what to pay attention to during the interview, what are the common types of written tests and other details, but also talk about how to do personal positioning, career planning, the difference between job hunting and job hunting and other macro issues.I hope this book can bring you a perfect job search journey from routines, skills to methods and rules, so that everyone can find a job 100% successfully.In addition, please pay attention to WeChat public number (Baihe Marketing Research Institute, ID: BHY X365) for more exciting content.If you still have any questions about job interview or marketing copy, please come to consult (knock signal: consultation).

Author He Bai

September 2019, Zhengzhou

First, what should be prepared before applying for a job

Cultivating good quality 1. Ideological and moral quality is the basic guarantee of professional success. Good quality will be transformed into noble professional ethics and firm belief in life in future jobs.2. Scientific and cultural quality.Work hard to learn scientific and cultural knowledge and lay a solid professional foundation.Having real talent and learning can adapt to more jobs and is more conducive to one's own employment.3. Physical quality is the material guarantee for professional success.College students should exercise scientifically, take an active part in sports activities, understand their own physiological quality characteristics and requirements of different professions, and rationally develop and utilize their own physiological advantages in future professional activities.4. Aesthetic quality is the basic quality that any profession should possess.Often enjoy excellent literary and artistic works, learn to identify good and evil, beauty and ugliness, and develop aesthetic ability. If one forms an artistic hobby and specialty, one will have a broader prospect for future employment.5. Labor quality is the foundation of operation ability and practice ability.Through labor, one can exercise one's body and will and acquire productive knowledge and labor skills.6. Good psychological quality is a necessary factor to win the competition.The high technology, high efficiency and high competition in today's society have increased people's psychological burden.People with good mentality, optimism and confidence, and correct treatment of setbacks may succeed.Second, to complete self-positioning, "self-positioning" means to find one's own position.You have to find out what you want to do (work)?What can you do?To find the combination of the two, on this basis to determine their own career goals, then to analyze the employment situation, find out the starting point of your career goals, that is, in which city, which industry and which type of position you are most likely to find a suitable job for you.The choice of profession should be considered in combination with the major studied. It is appropriate to choose this major. If there are other outstanding specialties besides the major, you can also choose across majors, but the span should not be too large.In terms of job selection, one may as well enter the job with a low profile. High standards, high starting point and high profile are difficult to realize in a buyer's market environment where the supply of graduates exceeds the demand.III. Preparation of Personal Data Personal data mainly includes personal resumes and relevant certification materials.Proof materials include: identification card, student card, employment recommendation form, etc.Academic record certification materials-school transcripts and specially issued certificates, etc.;The original and photocopy of the certificate-English and computer grade certificate, professional qualification certificate, award-winning certificate, etc. IV. Information collection and recruitment information can be obtained from the employment guidance center for school graduates, special supply and demand meetings arranged for graduates in various places, campus job fairs for well-known enterprises, newspapers, radio, television, Internet, SMS, and friends and relatives.Among them, the information from the school has the highest credibility.Note: After obtaining the recruitment information, attention should also be paid to the screening of the information, and it should be confirmed whether the recruitment unit exists, whether the recruitment activity is arranged, whether these people you meet are responsible for the recruitment, job positions, working hours, work place and treatment level are consistent with the recruitment information.Five, psychological preparation for job hunting is not a smooth road, bumping on the way is inevitable.Please remember that the ultimate goal of all difficulties in life is not to defeat you but to exercise you, improve you and seize the opportunity to temper yourself.Six, fast learning some practical interview skills, the key is how to introduce yourself in 1-3 minutes, how to show your advantages and strength as much as possible, and give the interviewer a reason to choose you.Be prepared for some common interview questions.It is better to do a simulated interview exercise, find a manager or supervisor in the enterprise among friends and relatives to make an on-site evaluation and make suggestions so as to find problems and adjust them in time.Keep in mind: a brief and prominent self-introduction is very important.In addition to general requirements such as professionalism, experience and dedication, different job types have different emphasis requirements.For example, marketing positions focus on communication, customer development and agility.Accounting focuses on rigour and principle.Technology R&D focuses on logicality and professionalism.Planning and creative positions focus on planning ability and divergent thinking.Engineering focuses on execution and practicality.Human resources focus on affinity, communication and motivation.Administrative services focus on service, enthusiasm and detail.However, middle and senior management positions focus on cognitive height, leadership, coordination and integration.Preparation before going to the interview 1. Dress decently and neatly.2. Check whether the materials needed for the interview are complete.3, estimate the journey time, must set aside rich time, not late, but also don't have to arrive too early.Before the interview and during the interview 1. Before the interview, tidy up your clothes and hair.2. Knock at the door and greet the examiner with a smile.The examiner motioned that the sitting position should be natural and graceful, and the sitting position should be correct.3, must be full of confidence, remember confidence is not necessarily successful, but not confident will fail.Be calm, positive, mature, and not nervous (only relax can you bring your own things into play), so as to make people feel that you are talented, professional and honest.Preparation of interview questions 1. Please talk about your own situation first.There are two ways to answer this question: one is to answer the question directly, which can answer one's greatest strengths, characteristics, professional skills, etc.Second, after a brief self-description, I quickly transferred the answer to my skills, experience and training for the current job.Why did you come to apply for this company?Candidates should generally prepare several more reasons before the interview, but the reasons should be brief and practical.In order to show the reason and working intention of the application, the answer should be related to the products and enterprises of the application company. It is better not to answer because there is room for development in the future and because the answer such as stability should show that the enterprise has been fully studied.How much do you know about our company?This is a question to test the applicant's interest in the company and his willingness to work in the company. Just answer a part of the company's brief introduction and the advertisement for personnel.What do you think of the current situation of this industry?This problem is mainly to understand the job seekers' understanding and prospect of the current industrial situation.For the inexperienced, it is to test his willingness and care for this job.Since I have just graduated from school, my knowledge in this field is only confined to books. I don't need to pretend to be an expert in front of the personnel manager, and I don't need to state any original opinions. All you have to do is pass on correct and true opinions.What is your work view?Don't think too complicated, you can answer "why do you work", "what do you get from your work", "what are my plans after n years" and so on.6. Why do you want to find such a position?If asked this question, this is what the other party wants to know, whether you belong to the kind of person who can only work in any company.If so, he would not be interested in you.Employers are looking for people who can solve problems at work. Such people work harder and more efficiently.Therefore, you can answer like this: "I have spent a lot of time designing my career. I think this kind of work is suitable for me, because many of the problems that this job requires are my hobbies and my strengths."7. Can you accept overtime?This is to examine your "enthusiasm for work".As a young man, he should show great attention and enthusiasm for his work.Of course, unreasonable overtime is not necessarily good, and the best answer is "if it is within the scope of their responsibilities, it is not overtime."What kind of treatment do you want?The best way is to give a clear and definite answer to the question of treatment.Objective induction of personal age, experience, ability, and then according to the industry category, company size and other objective information, put forward reasonable figures, but with the explanation of the reasons for improving treatment is very necessary.This is also a good opportunity to evaluate the applicant's ability and experience and show confidence.

After three years of college higher education and excellent culture, entering senior year, we began to directly face the upcoming peak of job hunting for fresh graduates.College time is really beautiful, but we can't live in an ivory tower all the time. We have to get out of the shelter, join in the society and give ourselves to the market.Needless to say, due to the impact of economic transformation and college enrollment expansion, college students' job hunting and employment has become a hot topic in the past two years.At present, the domestic employment situation is quite clear, and there is a clear gap between employers' employment plans and graduates' current situation in terms of both quantity and requirements.Finding a job or finding a satisfactory job is a big challenge for us who are approaching graduation.A realistic and well-thought-out job search plan is especially important for us who are going to be on the front line.2. Analysis of Employment Situation Dickens said in A Tale of Two Cities: "This is the best time, this is the worst time;This is the season of light and this is the season of darkness.This is the spring of hope and the winter of disappointment.People have all kinds of things in front of them and nothing in front of them. "These words also apply to the changeable IT industry.We are at the best of times.The vigorous development of China's economy has provided sufficient capital guarantee for the IT industry. From the introduction of technology to the independent innovation of technology, it is bound to cultivate new sources of power for China's economic growth in addition to factors such as system, resources and capital.In the take-off era of a country, IT professionals have the luck that no one before them can match.The economic growth momentum contained in the economic system reform is far from being released.The overall demand of information users will not change the upward trend. For IT industry, there should be more opportunities than other industries.Specifically, IT business upgrade requirements and new system construction support will promote the rapid development of IT software and hardware and system integration services, with the Internet, application development integration, and IT training and other market segments being more significantly promoted centrally.We are in the worst times.The reason why this is the worst time is that we are experiencing a "once-in-a-century" financial crisis. The possibility of global IT market recession triggered by this crisis is increasing.If we fail to grasp the opportunity of change and make a good plan for ourselves, the redistribution of wealth and the intensification of the butterfly effect will make people who fail to grasp the opportunity of this era face uncertainty.If the IT explosion in the early 21st century created the wealth myth of many investors, then the gradual regulation of the market in recent years has made many latecomers realize the bitter taste of the disappearance of the bubble.Whether it is the best time or the worst time depends on how we make use of it.There are always ups and downs in the industry, and mastering the road is an art that requires wisdom and patience.Third, the choice of job-hunting intention and the determination of one's own job-hunting intention can match one's ideal position with one's own.Combine one's major and one's own special skills, interests, hobbies and other personality characteristics to determine one's own job-hunting goals.The following analysis is based on my own personality and interests.First of all, I have a strong interest in software development, so I want to develop into a software engineer in the future.Personally, I prefer to study technology and other issues, so it is a good study habit for software development.For any profession, it is an eternal topic to continuously learn and enrich yourself.This is especially true for software engineers.I like to do in-depth research on technology, and I also like to constantly learn new technologies to enrich myself and keep up with the pace of the times.Secondly, I think the software engineer is a promising one.Especially in recent years, China's software industry has great opportunities.The demand for talents in the information technology and Internet industries has always been the highest in the whole year.The development level of software industry determines a country's information industry development level and its comprehensive competitiveness in the international market.The state will invest a lot of financial, material and human resources to train high-level software talents and develop related enterprises.I think this is a good opportunity. With the support of the state, the software industry will develop rapidly.Finally, the salary of software engineers is higher than that of other majors.Of course, it is mainly based on one's own ability.The most important thing is that software engineers have a lot of room for development in the future and are diversified.It is also possible to transfer from a software development engineer to an enterprise to do management work.Buy a good house and go to Zhengzhou for real estate sales-gather all the real houses on the net!Transparent quotation!Advertising selects a good house for you. Zhengzhou's real estate sales can be quoted through multiple channels. It's in the chain!Looking at Details > "Sales Department" Zhengzhou Real Estate New Building in Zhengzhou in August, the 92-154m^2 grand subscription plan advertised Zhengzhou real estate next to Huiji Wanda, "Line 2" 92-154m^2 high-rise/duplex villa "Garden+Basement Full Gift" Looking at Details > > 4. Intended target positions require major recruitment websites to have certain requirements for the position of software engineer.The general requirements are as follows: familiar with the basic knowledge of Java, the basic knowledge of database, the basic process of software development, English level 4 and above, and self-condition analysis: continuous professional scholarship, English level 4 and 6 certificates, understanding and mastering ICONIX software development process, and project experience.Can use programming languages such as C++/C#/Java/python, and can write high-quality C/S architecture programs, database programs, and WEB applications according to requirements documents and coding specifications.As a project manager, good at communicating with people, team and overall awareness, able to solve problems independently.Like to contact new things and new technologies.Positive in life, optimistic and cheerful, willing to help others.Willing to endure hardship, honest and sincere.6. Plan and Arrangement 1. Mentality Adjustment: First, make full understanding and psychological preparation, face up to reality, society and oneself.We should dare to endure setbacks, look to the future, and learn to look at employment from a developmental perspective.2. Resume: Combining one's education background, experience, specialty, hobbies and other relevant situations, one should make a decent and focused resume.3. Professional Quality Training: Before applying for a job, one should do a good job in professional quality training.Including etiquette, dress and other aspects of professional training.The essence is the conversion training of individual roles. In the process of job hunting, one must seriously and strictly treat one's own professional accomplishment, constantly learn and correct.4. Information Collection: Collect relevant recruitment information through various channels, including newspapers, posters, employment information network of online university employment guidance centers, and "double-selection" job fairs organized by universities and colleges.

Three, several common job search methods

If you want to enter an enterprise whose salary is determined by your strength, you'd better choose an enterprise in the early stage of growth, with more opportunities for promotion, but at a slightly slower pace.The system and system of enterprises in the later stage of growth are on track. I am afraid it is difficult to get promotion or salary increase in a short period of time. Most large enterprises belong to this stage.If you want to enter an enterprise with ordinary salary but high stability, you'd better choose an enterprise with mature period, but you should have psychological preparation, because your working career may be long and hard, and the possibility of promotion is small.1. Enterprises in recession don't need to consider unless you have extraordinary ability to revive enterprises that are on the verge of closing down. You don't need to fight with your immaturity.2. Each industry has its outstanding regional characteristics. The industry you choose may be unfamiliar here, lacking the realistic conditions and atmosphere for prosperity, but it is already in full swing and has become a new climate.In this case, you have to consider where to seek employment opportunities.3. To find the balance point between reality and ideal, when the reality conflicts with the ideal in mind, one should know how to choose and accept the result after making a decision. Behind remorse is meaningless torture of oneself and ruthless reduction of one's spirit.After determining the general direction, you should consider how to achieve your employment goals.The following are some representative job-hunting methods, as well as the characteristics and precautions of various job-hunting methods.Example: Trade-off and Trade-off The major I studied is now in small demand, so many of our classmates are facing the problem of professional mismatch.Whether this problem can be solved is closely related to the cultivation of personal qualities.At ordinary times, we should not only practice our foreign language skills, but also pay attention to the cultivation of Chinese and the dabbling of various knowledge. Our knowledge system has been enriched and our knowledge has been broadened. Only by doing so can we be suitable for more diverse lives and be more competent for our work in the future. I myself have encountered such problems.After I stepped up my efforts to find a job in the final stage, three units reached a preliminary intention with me.At that time, I was very hesitant, even confused, and did not know how to choose.Different people have different values, different inclinations towards the future, different specialities and so on, so they make different choices.I am very satisfied with two of the three units. One is a British-owned computer company. I go to the company to do editing work. The other is a large state-owned enterprise with a history of more than 100 years established during the Westernization Movement. I go to the unit to do translation work. I am satisfied with both units. I like both jobs. However, I cannot have both fish and bear's paw. Who should I give up?I chose the latter.The main reason is that there is very little demand for my major, so the chance of finding a job with a professional counterpart is very small.I have deep feelings for my major. If I miss this opportunity and will not be able to apply my major in the future, I will have no theory and no practice at all. I think it will be my lifelong regret.And the editing job I love, I may still have a chance in the future, so, although foreign companies may have high salaries and favorable treatment, I gave up and chose a professional counterpart job, although the working environment of state-owned enterprises may be depressing.I don't regret it, because I think it is a kind of happiness to be able to use my major in my work, to better show myself and to develop my skills.The wealth of life is not only measured by money, there are many things that are more precious and worth cherishing. I am glad that I have seized this opportunity.I. Job Hunting Methods (1) Online job hunting relies on the Internet. To be more precise, it is undoubtedly the unique way of today's times to get an interview through the Internet.There are so many network information that even the most outstanding talents may not be able to attract the full attention of employers.According to statistics, larger enterprises generally receive 500 to 1,000 e-resumes a week, 80% of which are deleted within 30 seconds of managers browsing.It is much more difficult to get others interested in you through an e-mail within half a minute than to meet directly with the employer.1, direct delivery resume for a job seeker, want to apply for a job on the Internet, the most important thing is to write your resume and cover letter.Many well-known human resources websites have provided resume writing templates for job seekers. In this case, the external appearance of a job seeker's resume is no different and cannot reveal the personality characteristics of the job seeker at all.Therefore, if you want to attract employers' attention, you should pay attention to the contents of your resume, show your uniqueness and potential as much as possible, which is the key step to success in job hunting.Do not send resumes frequently to the same organization.The validity period of online job search information is generally 30 to 60 days.Employers will actively prepare for follow-up work after the recruitment is released, so employers have a certain operating cycle.If your resume has not been answered for a week, it can be re-sent appropriately considering the safety of e-mail.However, never send job resumes and cover letters to the same organization frequently for three days and two ends, which will undoubtedly arouse the dislike of the other party.Don't apply for more than one position at the same time.In online job hunting, there are many job seekers applying for multiple positions at the same time.Applying for multiple positions at the same time in one unit does not show that you are superior in ability. You are a versatile person.On the contrary, the employer will think that you are blind when applying for a job, do not have your own set goals, are casual, unprofessional and lack integrity.According to one's specialty, hobbies, and specialties, as well as your pre-designed criteria for job position, place of work, and remuneration, etc., then rank qualified units according to these criteria, and apply to the employing units in a targeted way.Spreading resumes all over the internet is not only a waste of time, but also has little practical effect.When delivering your resume, be sure to give priority to the newly released recruitment information, so that you can have more confidence.For those positions that were released earlier and are still within the validity period, because they have been in progress for a period of time, the resumes received will certainly not be less, and no matter how much energy you put in, you will not necessarily have a good result.You can also log on to the employer's website directly. Generally speaking, the employment information they publish on their website is also relatively reliable.It is best not to send resumes as attachments.Although resumes sent in the form of attachments look better, due to the threat of viruses, more and more websites of organizations require job seekers not to send resumes in attachments.Even some units have deleted all the mails with attachments. It is also possible that due to technical reasons, some employers' computers cannot open the attachments, thus allowing good job opportunities to slip away in vain.Carefully design your resume in plain text format.Pay attention to setting the margins so that the width of the text is about 16cm, so that your resume will not appear to wrap in most cases.Try to use a larger font size;If you must make your resume look different, you can use some special symbols to separate the contents of your resume.Generally, published works or papers should not be attached to the e-resume, because Zhengzhou jiezhuang company _ has the possibility of spreading viruses through e-mail attachments. zhengzhou jiezhuang company chooses "have home decoration" as its advertisement. 23 years of decoration experience have been accumulated. well-known decoration design teams have tailored the decoration plan. check details > Zhengzhou decoration is afraid of trouble, choose love space, how to decorate extreme practical advertisement, how to decorate love space-including whole house, package construction, from blank to hardcover, E0 grade environmental protection, and there are no additions in the whole process!View details > has always existed.In addition, employers generally do not read the attached works carefully.When applying for different positions in the same company, it is best to send two different e-resumes, because some job search websites' database software can automatically filter out the second identical letter to avoid redundancy.To miss the rush hour, send your e-resume.The peak time for surfing the Internet is usually from noon to midnight. The transmission speed is very slow during this period, and error messages will also appear. Therefore, it is necessary to choose the right time to move.After sending out the job application materials, you should actively contact the employer.Ask the employer about the situation through E-mail or telephone, show sincerity to the employer, and let oneself know fairly well.If you want your resume to hit a higher rate, you can take some time to do some research on the more suitable positions and employers through the web page, and then write a few tailor-made job-seeking statements in front of your resume to show your understanding of the industry and enterprises, the importance you attach to the job, and your respect for the recipients.In the subject column of the email, it is best to write a short sentence, which indicates both the job-hunting position and the advantages of one's own application, so that the probability of being selected will be greatly increased.Some small flaws you inadvertently left in the process of applying for a job online are sometimes enough to make people judge against you.Due to the error-prone nature of online recruitment, extra care is needed, such as sending carefully prepared resumes from one organization to another in a hurry, or mispronounced words. The result is certainly conceivable.The online application form must be filled out according to the requirements designed by the recruitment company, and the words must be carefully chosen.If you are not sure, you'd better write it down online in advance to ensure the quality of the filling.If you have a favorite unit, you may as well go to its website first.Employers will not miss any chance to hunt for outstanding talents.In order to provide convenience for online resume delivery, they will show humanistic considerations in the design of web pages.On the front pages of these organizations' websites, nine out of ten will have job opportunities or join us.Click to enter the corresponding page, you can see the details of existing recruitment positions and recent recruitment activities.Some units will also introduce the relevant contents of employee management in detail on the website, such as performance management, training opportunities, corporate culture, etc. Through these contents, you can have a fuller understanding of these units.Direct contact with the unit is more direct and has a higher probability of success.It is recommended to use the job search mailbox provided by the website.Large domestic human resources websites generally set up special recruitment mailboxes for enterprises that publish information.If you are interested in a certain position, when you check the specific job description and requirements, a prompt will usually appear on the page to apply for the position. Click on the prompt and your resume will be sent automatically.This avoids the contradiction that you cannot send it effectively because the mailbox of the employer is not large enough.However, the prerequisite for enjoying this service is that your resume must have been registered on the website.Don't expect only one fixed phone to be enough, it is better to leave two moments to find you or to tell your contact information.Also don't expect each contact method to be tried by the other party, such as e-mail, it is better to stay than not to stay, but when you open the mailbox, you will find that the other party's reply is not many, and the organizations that notify you of the interview often choose the telephone method at the same time.Some units do not have any vacant positions or recruitment plans at present, but if you are very fond of it, you can still fill in a job application form, perhaps the HR of this unit will save your data into the talent pool.Perhaps they have read your information and think you are excellent and suitable for them, thus giving you a special opportunity.1. The online application letter is best to tailor a resume for each recruitment enterprise you like, and then write a sincere application letter in front of your resume and send it together.Even if you fill in a job application form online, don't forget to send another cover letter.The cover letter and resume should be in text format to facilitate the personnel supervisor to read.

Four, how to do a good job resume

How to make a good resume is, as the name implies, a simple resume.When we want to condense our goals, advantages and strength into a small piece of A4 paper, most people feel perplexed, disconsolate because of their rich experience, or anxious because they have very little experience.So, what factors should an excellent resume have?What advice does HR have for making resumes?If you are trying to get an interview, you may as well calm down and look down.Why are you?Why me?After years of ideological indoctrination, most job seekers have the awareness that HR has a rather limited time to read each resume, spending 15 seconds cursorily browsing resumes while reading resumes of interest for less than 120 seconds.So, what is HR's benchmark for judging "unqualified", "qualified" or "excellent" resumes in such a short period of time?Jessica, Dell (China) Human Resources Manager, believes that a good resume is nothing more than a job seeker's high awareness of himself and his target position.Which is why you? Why me?-the famous pri (position-relevant information) principle.What soft qualities do the enterprise need from you? These soft qualities should be reflected in your resume and the other party should be removed from the resume.Only when the resume highly meets the recruitment requirements can the job seeker obtain the interview opportunity.This also reminds us that we should not only have a resume template.However, at present, more than 62% still have only one resume template.Details determine success or failure. Some details in resumes are often ignored by us. Jessic believes that these details are not absolute factors for a good resume, but will definitely affect the interview opportunity.Basic Information: The contact phone number should be kept open for 12 hours. If the phone number is "empty", "busy" or "not in the service area", HR will make another call, but this is not absolute.As long as the home address indicates the specific location, the protection of personal privacy can be fully reflected at this time.The residence should be consistent with the location of the target enterprise to reduce the enterprise's worries about cost control.Job-hunting intention: I hope that the industry and the target location are the same as those of the target enterprise.The number of target functions should not exceed 5, and they should be relevant to avoid "unclear target" of resumes.Education experience: only from the highest degree or university degree.Awards should be selectively included according to the nature of the target position.If you apply for a software engineer, you should avoid such descriptions as "getting the third place in high jump in high school".Training experience and certificates: for college students, computer certificates and English level certificates are bonus points;For professionals with certain working experience, internal training experience and registration certificate will directly affect promotion, salary increase and even job-hopping opportunities.(The above fields are previously called 51job standard resume template fields, which are also common fields for HR screening resumes in the recruitment system.) Three points are grasped in the description of work experience: keyword number results. It is no exaggeration to say that the first 15 seconds of HR resume review time is given to the work experience column.Only when the work experience meets the requirements of the position will HR spend 100 seconds to deeply read personal related data including personal information, self-evaluation, educational experience, etc.Therefore, the quality of job experience description determines the chances of getting an interview.So, how can "work experience" look attractive?How to display the working ability with the most effective information under the limited resource constraints?Worry-free experts suggest: to avoid using a straightforward tone to describe work experience, but to follow the "key words, numbers, results" principle.Speak with Key Words: What are Key Words?Common keywords include "team consciousness, creativity, stress resistance" and so on, which can be obtained from job recruitment information released by enterprises.Some positions have specific keywords, such as "marketing awareness, acceleration" and so on.Since HR's top 15 browsing of resumes is actually a scan of keywords, Jessica suggests that more time can be spent to find potential keywords for the position.Speaking with Numbers: The brain is more sensitive to the reception and transmission of digital information, and quantifying the ability to work can make the abstract description of ability clearer.For example, we can try to change "excellent written expression and communication ability" to "wrote a glossary guide for 1500 users."Speak in terms of results:

results are performance, and we should make it to a certain extent in the description of results in the resume.For example, we can try to change "cases that have been successful in analyzing customer needs" to "create and implement a comprehensive needs assessment mechanism to help predict demand for services and employees."This year's graduates focus on creating two points in their resume writing: the job information released by internship organizations and enterprises all require job seekers to have more or less working experience, which is undoubtedly a major weakness for this year's graduates.Resumes of fresh graduates need to emphasize internship experience and community activity to highlight their social practice ability.Speaking in terms of internship: Jessica said that students can try to practice some positions during their sophomore year. quite a number of well-known enterprises have campus recruitment activities and students should actively participate in them.The higher the popularity of internship enterprises, the higher the take-off height after graduation.In the face of job hunting, if the internship experience is quite excellent, the average score of subjects may become a secondary condition.   Jessica recalled: "When Chengdu University of Electronic Science and Technology recruits sales internship positions, the starting point required is very high as the applicants will be directly assigned to work in Xiamen for half a year-the average score of subjects should be above 85 points, English should pass at least six levels, and relevant social experience and so on are required.We received about 2,000 resumes in one night, of which 400 or 500 were selected, one of which attracted me especially.The average score of this student's subject is only 80 points, and his English has only passed Band 4.His internship experience described it like this:' I once sold digital cameras in an electrical appliance city in Chengdu, and I adopted three strategies (concrete) at that time, exceeding 200% of the target and defeating the classmates who sold SONY in the same group.'Although he had many hard conditions that did not meet the standards, he was very organized and highlighted his experiences and achievements.Therefore, we gave the boy an interview.In the end, we accepted him. The following year, he became an excellent salesman. We sent him to join a top sales club in Dubai at that time."Speak in terms of community activity: for example, once served as president of a community, sometimes it means having leadership ability.Once held community activities, sometimes it means having the ability to organize, coordinate, negotiate, team work, etc.HR often maps small associations to large enterprises. By transferring the environment, HR will think that students' performance in associations is also established in enterprises.Therefore, in the university, we can't miss not only love, but also internship and community activities.Cross-industry resume emphasizes three points: language ability, soft skills, target industry cognition, as the saying goes: interlacing is like mountains.Cross-bank has little impact on financial and administrative posts, but for technical and market posts, the barriers to new lines can be large or small.When the accumulated work experience is wasted due to cross-line, the enterprise will not buy the full-time account.We should carefully plan our careers to avoid becoming a monk halfway through the year.However, when there is always a plan to keep up with changes, we can add weight to the resume from three aspects: foreign language ability, soft skills and target industry awareness in order to increase personal competitiveness as a last resort.Highlight foreign language skills: the number of languages or proficiency level are all gold supplements for resumes."Proficient in professional languages", "Familiar with the cultural customs of a country" and "Mastering three or five languages" are still good selling points today.Outstanding soft skills: soft skills are intangible, emotional and uncertain.Such as a person's communication ability, analysis ability, interpersonal relationship, leadership coordination ability, there are some potential and ability to be developed.Research shows that the more senior positions are developed, the more obvious the proportion of soft skills is.The target industry has high awareness: this is the only way to highlight that you are not an outsider.A clear-cut industry report is enough to get a job, but only if there is a real need for recruitment.For the latest information on a certain industry, please refer to the worry-free industry index.However, we should realize that for cross-travelers, resumes are always green leaves and contacts are the real red flowers.

Five, resume job intention how to write

Job-hunting intention, which literally means the direction of job-hunting, is to plan one's career according to one's hobbies and abilities, and to define one's occupation so as to find a suitable job.Job-hunting intentions may include: the nature of the intended job (full-time/part-time), the job industry, the place of work, the position and the salary.Job-seeking intention is the core of a resume, that is, the soul of a resume. The rest of the resume revolves around this core.Clarifying one's job-hunting intention is the first step in finding a job, so that when looking for a job, one can follow this direction and find a suitable position in a targeted way.To determine the job-hunting intention, one must first start from one's own character, interests, abilities, values, etc. to find one's own suitable position, which is also a typical self-cognition problem.Then, learn more about the job you are looking for.On the basis of knowing one's enemy and one's self, one can make one's own job-hunting decision.Method 1. The best writing method for job-hunting intention should be: industry+job title or precise job title, such as sales work in communication field;Or, for example, web page design and network maintenance.Mechanical professionals can consider positions such as mechanical design, mechanical engineer, and drawing.Such a description is more in line with HR's psychology of quick screening, and only such a description can bring you more interview opportunities.2. The intention to apply for a job should be clearly stated.Be sure to clearly write your personal profile on the front page.Because most enterprises may have more than one job at the same time when recruiting, and HR is very fast when looking at resumes, and the first thing to look at is job intention.If you don't clearly write your job intention in a conspicuous position, it is generally easy to be ignored by HR.3. In your resume, be sure to indicate your intention to apply for a job.When writing job-seeking intentions, remember that there is a vague phenomenon, such as hoping to engage in challenging work.Also don't fill in too much personal resume._ advertising with the intelligent resume tool recommended by senior HR is an excellent resume production platform in China. it provides a large number of exquisite resume templates for downloading and online production of resumes. see details > 2019 how to write a new recruitment clerk _ how to edit a recruitment clerk online _ how to write a PSD-free advertisement for a recruitment clerk?2 million templates are directly modified online, and the replacement text will be plotted. how to write the recruitment clerk _ click to use it. check the details > there are too many miscellaneous items, such as clerks, assistants, administration, personnel, etc. there is no pertinence, so people do not know what you can do.The content of the resume should focus on the job-seeking intention, and the irrelevant content should be omitted as far as possible.Job-hunting Intention Fan Wen Dear Leader: Hello!First of all, thank you for looking up my information in your busy schedule. Here I would like to accept your selection with the true side of a graduating student.As a software major student, I love my major.And constantly improve themselves, beyond themselves, in order to accumulate knowledge, find a suitable position in your unit, with the highest efficiency as the unit to create more efficiency, realize their own value in life.

Six, job considerations

What factors should be considered in choosing a career?Here is a 360-degree full-view analysis to share with you.I hope this article is helpful to those students who are preparing to find a job and are still in a period of confusion.At the heart of the job are three elements: industry, company and position.The following contents are written according to the order of importance usually considered by the general public. Since different people expect different weights in different aspects, the following can only represent the consideration of most people. If there are individual requirements for work, it will vary from person to person.As shown in the figure: ... (1) external perspective-job selection: [51Job]- without worries about future]-nearby job information, hot job search/recruitment on the job search website!Advertising 51job recruitment website, professional recruitment website, a large number of popular job recruitment information, free registration to fill in resume, easy to find a job.Advertisements apply for jobs, go online, 250,000 headhunters recommend good jobs, help you easily get offer, and update a large number of high-paying positions in real time!There are many ways to define and classify work.For example, the eyes of Guanghua students in Peking University are: first-class people go into investment banks, second-class people go into consulting, and third-class people go into the top 500.In the eyes of many entrepreneurs, the top 500 are the places that die the fastest and are most unfavorable to talent development and entrepreneurship.In the eyes of many professional managers, the top 500 is the best starting point for graduating from college.Therefore, all kinds of viewpoints should be listened to. The key is to find out why people say so and what the reason is.It is very important to learn to synthesize multiple perspectives.Industry prospect: industry is always more important than company.Perhaps you have entered a very good company, but it is in a sunset industry, which is also very tragic.For example, you have entered the best computer repair shop in the country.However, the maintenance industry has been declining more and more. The arrival of the consumer era has led to the direct abandonment of old articles and no longer repair them. Then your shoe repair shop is in a big industrial environment called repair and will not have much development.More realistically, the industry that we college students often consider, such as the retail industry, is worth considering, because the sales mode of e-commerce is gradually replacing the retail channel, and the growth of channel profit space is limited.Of course, retail in third-to fifth-tier cities is still the main mode, while large-scale retail like IKEA will continue to exist for a long time.Therefore, these thoughts need to be understood and judged by themselves.For example, many industries in China are growing rapidly now.Many miracles have taken place in the Internet industry and IT industry. Some very small start-up Internet enterprises have their own core technologies or other resources, and have huge potential for development and can learn a lot. This is the first choice for the "Challenge to Life" model (mentioned later), although they have low salaries and certain risks.While others, such as energy, chemical industry and medicine, have a steady growth momentum and can have better development.Emerging industries have endless opportunities, so we must seize them.Finance is naturally the pyramid of all trades, but unfortunately you have to have the skills to get jobs. and depending on what you do, at the bottom of the pyramid, the working hours are not necessarily proportional to the returns.On the other hand, as the saying goes, you will win the championship in every field. The main purpose here is to make sure that you are not going to a sunset industry and that you are also interested in this industry. That is still a good choice.Positioning-Ranking in Subdivision Industry: The focus here is on the idea of continuous subdivision.In general, the company that enters the first industry is always better than the second.At the same time, we should also learn to consider from another angle, that is, it is also very good if we can be the first in a subdivision industry.For example, TP-Link, although IT is not ranked first and second in IT enterprises, is ranked first in the field of terminal wireless network equipment, with a national market share of 70%, far ahead of any competitor, the world ranking has also risen to the top three, and the overseas market has a broad prospect.If you study and work in a company that ranks first in the industry, you will hopefully become an expert in a subdivision of the industry.And the more skilled the talent, the higher the radiation value.To give another familiar example of fast fading, Procter & Gamble is the first in the field of fast fading, but it is not the first in every category. Generally speaking, shampoo is a better department, and its four shampoo brands occupy four of the top five in China's shampoo market.And if you enter Unilever, then try to choose their fist products, such as Lipton, then you are also an expert under the first brand in the tea industry in China's fast-moving industry.Although Colgate cannot compete with Procter & Gamble, if you aspire to be a toothpaste expert, it will be a good choice.Of course, what I'm saying here is very general. To enter the company, you need to have a deeper position, for example, a marketing expert of 360 full-effect toothpaste series in the toothpaste field, or a research and development expert of high-purity extraction of silicon components in the toothpaste field?Another example is GE and IBM, which had friends working as interns before. There will be many departments, for example GE has finance.

Seven, job interview self-introduction Fan Wen 3 minutes

Dear leaders: Good morning, everyone!First of all, I am very honored to stand here and take part in the interview. I thank all leaders for giving me this interview opportunity!My name is xxx and I graduated from xx College majoring in nursing.In my mind, nursing is a sacred, noble and great profession. Nurses are extraordinary people in ordinary posts.This sacred profession has been my ideal since childhood. With constant pursuit of the ideal, I have finally ushered in today's starting point.In a twinkling of an eye, three years of college life have passed quietly.In the past three years, I have been enthusiastic about the nursing career, insisting on learning as the main task, and have achieved good results. I have been rated as an outstanding student cadre, an advanced individual with self-reliance and self-improvement and an outstanding university graduate.In addition to my study, I also did not forget to enrich my extra-curricular knowledge, participated in various extra-curricular activities and part-time jobs, participated in the national computer secondary training and obtained the qualification certificate.Through two years of theoretical study in school and one year of clinical practice in hospital, I have mastered the basic abilities that a nurse should possess, and at the same time, I have established such important concepts as love, responsibility and collective honor that a nurse should possess.Facing the new environment, new starting point and new challenges, I will do my best.Finding a way to succeed, not an excuse for failure, is my motto.I know that to become an excellent nursing worker, I must constantly improve myself. Therefore, while studying theoretical knowledge, I also applied for the undergraduate self-study examination of Chongqing Medical University to improve my academic qualifications.Finally, I sincerely thank the leaders for giving me this interview opportunity.If I am lucky enough to be a member of your hospital, I will devote myself to nursing work with full enthusiasm and repay your hospital's kindness with my sweat, knowledge and enthusiasm.I firmly believe that your trust will become the driving force for me to work harder!Thank you.

Eight, the domestic more reliable recruitment website

Disadvantages of the old recruitment websites: they have fallen into decline, have poor support for IT industry recruitment, and even do not have a special game industry recruitment.Not recommended.LinkedIn has the following advantages: the quality of human resources is high, and the quantity is also of a certain scale. As long as there are people with accounts, there is always a way to find any one of them and recommend headhunters.Disadvantages: hr needs to spend a lot of time searching for the right person, and then try every means to get in touch with the candidate for a time, otherwise it cannot get contact information.It is too time consuming and inefficient.2. If the advantages of the neighboring network are: the Chinese version of the social recruitment platform can be searched, positions can be published, and few resumes are received, but the quality is higher than that of Zhilian and 51 resumes received.Disadvantages: The overall data of talents is much less. hr and job seekers need to pay close attention to each other to obtain contact information. Both hr and job seekers have relatively low utilization rate of the platform. Often the people I see or contact or pay attention to have logged in a long time ago.3. advantages of dajie network: it is very useful to recruit fresh graduates. fresh graduates are rich in resources, efficient in recruitment and convenient to contact.There is no charge for small and medium-sized recruitment.Disadvantages: It is only applicable to the recruitment of fresh graduates. If mature staff are recruited, the effect is not ideal.3. Vertical recruitment on the Internet 1. Advantages of the Internet: Internet recruitment supports better results and the quality of resumes received is generally good.Recommended in Beijing!Disadvantages: The supporting area is relatively limited, and the use effect of cities outside Beijing is generally good.2. Advantages over the Internet: community of marketing personnel and gathering place of professional marketing personnel.The quality of talents is relatively high, and the talents of senior sales and management are its highlights. The Internet recruitment support effect is relatively good. It is recommended to be used in Jiangsu, Zhejiang and Shanghai regions.Disadvantages: The platform is relatively new and there is less support for the recruitment industry.3. Advantages of employment: A bit like the recruitment tool recommended by cloud headhunters, it is very professional.The support to the Internet and game industry is relatively good, the quality of talents is relatively high, and the success rate of interview is good. It is recommended to use!Disadvantages: The support for first-tier cities is effective, but the recruitment for second-tier cities seems to have not been carried out yet.4. Advantages of Pangguo Network: In the place where professional talents gather, there are many skilled talents and geeks, and even talents that headhunters cannot reach.Disadvantages: First, expensive!Secondly, job seekers' intentions are generally weak, communication costs are high, and success rate is low.4. headhunting platform 1. advantages of the recruitment network: there are many high-quality resumes of candidates, and a pool of senior professional and technical and management talents, which are recommended for friends with medium and high-end recruitment needs.Disadvantages: After using it for a period of time, it is found that job seekers are generally impetuous in mentality, not steadfast in their desire to apply for jobs, low in success rate of interview and interview, and high in recruitment cost.2. Advantages of Zhaopin of Zhilian: The high-end platform similar to Zhaopin launched by Zhilian is also relatively complete in the industry and has high quality of talents, with senior sales and management talents as its highlights.Disadvantages: the platform is relatively new, the implementation time is not very long, the current use of job seekers and enterprises are not many, the overall impact is not high.Young people are confused and confused in their careers. The problem is not that they are not aware of the problem, but that they are aware of the problem and cannot find a solution to it.They do not know how to think about the future, nor do they know where the direction is, nor do they know how to find the direction.Let the past you, meet the future you, you have only one life, no experience and no way to start over. For the future, the biggest problem is not unpredictability, but unconsciousness and deliberate avoidance. If you do not make a choice for the future now, others will make a choice for you in the future, and you have no choice. For career planning, the biggest problem is not not not to plan, but not to carry out.Only in this way can we find a good job!

Nine, job interview common questions answer skills

1. Would you please introduce yourself?Answer hint: The average person answers this question too often, only saying the name, age, hobbies, and work experience, which are all on the resume.In fact,

what the enterprise most wants to know is whether the job seeker is competent for the job, including: the strongest skills, the most in-depth study of knowledge areas, the most positive part of personality, the most successful things done, the main achievements, etc. These can be unrelated to learning or related to learning. However, the enterprise will believe in them only if it emphasizes the positive personality and the ability to do things.Enterprises attach great importance to a person's courtesy. job seekers should respect the examiner and say "thank you" after answering each question. enterprises like polite job seekers.2. What do you think is the greatest advantage of your personality?Answer hint: Calm, clear-cut, firm, tenacious, helpful and caring, adaptable and humorous, optimistic and friendly.After one to two years of training and project practice in Peking University, plus internship, I am suitable for this job.1. What advantages do you think you have and what jobs do you think you are more suitable for?Reference answer: There is no standard answer to this question. Candidates should respond according to their own situation. The following are some advantages and their corresponding jobs for candidates' reference.First, introverted, conscientious, suitable for secretarial and accounting work;Second, she is extroverted, good at communication and suitable for public relations and marketing.Third, diligent and studious, good at summing up, suitable for teaching and scientific research work;Fourth, a strong sense of responsibility, good at helping others, suitable for service and security work;Fifth, being impartial and impartial, doing things fairly is suitable for law enforcement and administrative work.Sixth, to bear hardships and stand hard work, love one's post and be dedicated to one's work is the basis for doing all work well.Seventh, harmony with people and obedience to leadership are prerequisites for doing all work well.Eighth, professional competence and a combination of learning and application are the conditions for doing all work well.Ninth, adapting to the environment and being modest and eager to learn are the essential factors for doing all the work well.What is your specialty?Reference answer: There is no standard answer to this question. Candidates should respond according to their own situation. The following are descriptions of several specialties for candidates' reference.First, my personality is more gentle and quiet, treats people warmly, is polite, handles affairs steadily earnestly, has the dedication to work.I think this specialty has laid a foundation for office and secretarial work.Second, I have strong computer operation ability. I have passed the computer level 2 (or other level) examination. I like programming and have some knowledge of computer network and office automation. I think this specialty is one of the necessary skills for civil servants.Zhengzhou _ correction glasses _ headquarters support _ one person can do advertising correction glasses, headquarters support, one person can, open a shop is simple, check the details > Zhengzhou glasses shop to see my own experience of opening glasses shop!Advertising Zhengzhou glasses shop, choose word-of-mouth brand, can open a shop to take goods directly from manufacturers, check the details > third, I am good at writing, writing a solid foundation (if published articles can be listed), writing is one of the basic skills of official business;Fourth, I have special skills in sports (what are my special skills, what grades and certificates I have obtained) and what grade of driver's license I have for driving a vehicle. I think several special skills are helpful for doing a good job as a civil servant.Fifth, foreign languages (or other languages) have special skills (what grades and certificates have they obtained). With the progress of reform and opening up, my special skills will be useful in the future.Sixth, I have strong language skills and speak Putonghua well. I think this specialty is one of the basic skills necessary to do a good job in civil service.Can you talk about your shortcomings?Reference answer: there is no standard answer to this question, the examinee should answer according to his own situation, the key is to answer the shortcomings not only according to his own actual situation, but also to avoid the characteristics of this post, to convert the shortcomings into advantages, the following are several answers for the shortcomings, candidates reference.First, I am not very good at communicating too much, especially it is difficult to communicate with strangers.Although this is a shortcoming, it shows that you are cautious in making friends.Second, I am rather rigid in handling affairs, and sometimes I tend to be truer than others.Although this is a shortcoming, it shows that you are more in compliance with the established work standards of the unit and have certain principles.Third, I want to learn anything or major, but I have not learned anything.Although this is a shortcoming, it shows that you love learning and have a wide range of knowledge.Fourth, I am relatively slow to accept new lifestyles or popular things in society.Although this is a shortcoming, it shows that you are more traditional and do not blindly follow the trend.Fifth, I tend to put forward different opinions on people or things that I think are wrong, resulting in frequent offending.Although this is a shortcoming, it shows that you are more independent and principled.Sixth, I am more urgent and sometimes not accurate enough.Although this is a shortcoming, it shows that you finish your work faster.Seventh, I think much about the difficulties in my work and ask less from colleagues or leaders.Although this is a shortcoming, it shows that you have a strong ability to complete work tasks independently.What will you do if you encounter setbacks?Reference answer: First, we should have a correct understanding of setbacks.Many people's good ideas when their career is successful and plain sailing are actually very difficult to achieve. To accept such a reality, a person's life cannot be plain sailing. Behind success there will be many hardships, pains and even setbacks. It is normal to encounter some setbacks during a period of life. Only the accumulation of experience and knowledge can shape a successful person. Many great successful people have experienced setbacks (for example).Second, we should dare to face it. We should climb from where we fall down, do not fear difficulties, and dare to challenge them.Third, we should carefully analyze the causes of failure and find out the source. As the saying goes, failure is the mother of success. We should master the lessons from setbacks and provide experience for the next rise. We should also strengthen our study in normal working chemistry. One's life is limited and it is impossible to experience everything. We should learn from other people's experience. Finally, we may not have a particularly good way to deal with setbacks because of the fans of the authorities or the lack of knowledge and experience. This is to ask our relatives and friends to help us overcome the difficulties. We can use our collective efforts to purchase at a low price and over value.Advertising polarizer prices, Tmall Electric City, explosions low prices!Personal care, brand direct operation, leisurely and affordable, wayward piece by piece!See details > Honeywell goggles prices come to Shanghai for free!Goggles price spot promotion!Advertising professional goggles prices are available from stock. Bagu \ Honeywell Goggles Prices Shanghai Changwei, Goggles Prices Preferential Promotion!See details > 5. what is your greatest weakness?Answer hint: The enterprise has a high probability of asking this question, and usually does not want to hear what are the disadvantages of a direct answer. If the job seeker says that he is narrow-minded, jealous, lazy, temperamental and inefficient, the enterprise will definitely not employ you.Never answer "my greatest weakness is to be too perfect" smartly. some people think that such an answer will make them look better, but in fact, he is already in danger.Enterprises like job seekers to start with their own advantages, add some minor shortcomings in the middle, and finally turn the problem back to the advantages and highlight the advantages. Enterprises like smart job seekers.What do you think of overtime?Answer hint: In fact, many companies ask this question, but it doesn't prove that they must work overtime. They just want to test whether you are willing to contribute to the company.Answer sample: I have to work overtime if my job requires me. I am single now and have no family burden. I can devote myself to my job.But at the same time, I will also improve work efficiency and reduce unnecessary overtime.7. What are your salary requirements?Answer hint: If you have too low a salary requirement, it obviously belittles your ability.If you ask too much for salary, it will appear that you are overweight and the company cannot afford it.Some employers usually set a budget in advance for the position they are looking for, so the price they offer for the first time is often the highest price they can offer. They ask you just to confirm whether the money is enough to arouse your interest in the job.Answer Sample 1: I have no hard and fast salary requirements. I believe your company will be friendly and reasonable in handling my problems.I focus on finding the right job opportunities, so as long as the conditions are fair, I won't care too much.Answer Sample 2: I have been trained in systematic software programming and do not need a lot of training. Moreover, I am particularly interested in programming.Therefore, I hope the company can give me a reasonable salary according to my situation and market standard.Answer Sample 3: If you have to specify the number yourself, please do not say a wide range, then you will only get the minimum number.It is better to give a specific figure, which shows that you have made a survey of today's talent market and know the value of employees with academic qualifications like yourself.8. What is your career plan in five years?Answer hint: This is a question that every applicant does not want to be asked, but almost everyone will be asked, and the more common answer is "manager".However, in recent years, many companies have established special technical channels.These positions are often called "consultants", "consulting technicians" or "senior software engineers" and so on.Of course, it is also possible to name other positions that you are interested in, such as product sales manager, production manager and other jobs with relevant background in your major.You know, examiners always like aggressive candidates. If you say "I don't know" at this time, you may lose a good opportunity.